Beans

white Kidney ✓
Red Kidney ✓
White ✓
Pinto ✓
Black Turtle
White Pea Beans ✓
Red (small) ✓
Northern
Navy ✓

Red Chili Beans ✓
Great Northern ✓
Pinto ✓
small white ✓
Chickpeas ✓
Black-eyed Peas ✓

Peas

Vegan Protein Bowls

One Dish Protein Packed Meals For The Everyday Herbivore

Emily Walker

Cheezy quinoa millet bowl with spinach, beans and corn

Mexican millet salad

Bulgur tabbouleh with aromatic herbs

Roasted winter vegetable and millet salad

Pomegranate-bulgur salad

Protein packed plant-based meatballs

Gingered millet with japanese veggies

Matcha chia pudding with sweet dukkah

Bulgur vegetable chili

Lunch of millet, black beans, avocado and smoky paprika tahini

15 minute brussels sprout & tempeh stir-fry

General tso's tempeh

Roasted root vegetable salad with millet

Vegan asian orange tempeh

Mediterranean-inspired vegetables over millet

Coconut curried skillet farro and chickpeas with smoky potatoes

Mexican tempeh quinoa salad

Peanut butter basil tempeh with broccoli

Oriental bulgur-lentil-salad

Balsamic roasted brussels sprouts with polenta

Tempeh cauliflower butternut in teriyaki sauce

Butternut, barley & lentil pilaf

Sesame kale glow bowl

Three bean barley chili

Scrambled tempeh with watercress

Roasted butternut squash carrot barley farro sorghum quinoa

salad

Quinoa and cauliflower salad with popped sorghum

Barley risotto with fava beans and mushrooms

Tropical chia coconut-mango granola

Simple sorghum arugula salad with gluten-free rye croutons
roasted cauliflower & barley bowl

Vegan korean nourish bowl with barley (bibimbap)

Crock pot lentils with curry

Sorghum chickpea bowl

Chili-lime popped sorghum

Sorghum and roasted summer vegetable salad with tarragon and
basil

Lentils with roasted beets and carrots

Roasted red pepper, cauliflower & walnut buckwheat salad

Thai peanut curry lentils
buckwheat risotto with mushrooms & hazelnut cream

Healing moroccan lentil soup

Buckwheat mushroom risotto

Cauliflower salad with chickpeas, baby kale, cumin, lemon &
toasted buckwheat

Overnight coconut buckwheat porridge

Buckwheat risotto with spinach and mushrooms

General tso's chickpeas

Roasted eggplant coconut curry

Vegan butter chicken

Kung pao chickpeas

Buffalo chickpea mac 'n' cheese

Vegan creamy kale soup with spicy roasted chickpeas

Chickpea curry pot pies

Creamy curried kale and chickpeas

Cheezy quinoa millet bowl with spinach, beans and corn

Serves: 3

Ingredients
Quinoa
1 cup quinoa
¼ cup millets
2 cups vegetable broth/water
Other ingredients
1 tablespoon extra light olive oil
1 small yellow onion
1 clove garlic
½ cup frozen corn
4-5 fresh shiitake mushrooms
A large handful baby spinach
½ teaspoon himalayan/sea salt
¼ cup vegan mozzarella cheese (i used trader joe's vegan mozzarella style shreds)
1 can pinto beans, drained and rinsed
2 tablespoons hemp hearts
1 teaspoon garlic powder
1 teaspoon onion powder
1 teaspoon dried oregano
½ teaspoon dried thyme
A few sprinkles red pepper flakes

Instructions
Quinoa: turn the heat on high and bring the quinoa and broth to a boil, for about 4-6 minutes. Then, turn the heat to medium low (3-4) and simmer for about 20-25 minutes until the quinoa and millets are cooked.
Vegetables: be sure to wait a little while and have the quinoa almost cooked before starting.

Finely dice the onion into little cubes and chop the garlic into small pieces. Put it in the frying pan with a tablespoon of extra light olive oil.

Meanwhile, remove the stem from the shiitake mushrooms and dice it into small pieces and combine it with the corn. Slice your baby spinach into strips and set them aside.

Turn the heat on medium high (5-6) and cook the onions for about 12 minutes, then add the corn and shiitake mushrooms. Cook for another 3 minutes and add the spinach and salt. Stir it around for a couple of minutes.

Then, add the cooked quinoa, vegan mozzarella cheese, the pinto beans (drain them, rinse with water and drain very well before adding), hemp hearts, garlic powder, onion powder, oregano, thyme and red pepper flakes.

Stir and make sure everything is even. Cook for a final 6 minutes and serve.

Mexican millet salad

Yield-2 cups
Total time-30 mins
Ingredients
1 cup millet
2 tablespoons olive oil
1/2 yellow onion, diced
1/2 green pepper, diced
1 cup black beans, drained and rinsed
2 plum tomatoes, deseeded and diced
1/4 bunch fresh cilantro, chopped ← parsley
Salt and pepper to taste
Queso fresco, to taste

Instructions
Cook millet as package recommends (1 cup millet to 2 cups water is the ratio).

While millet is cooking, over medium high heat sauté the onion, pepper, and black beans for about 5 minutes, until onions are tender.

Place cooked vegetables and beans in a bowl, toss with tomatoes and chopped cilantro. Add cooked millet and season to taste.

Great serve either warm or cold with a sprinkling of queso fresco.

Quinoa Bulgur Tabbouleh with Aromatic Herbs – *No*
Serves 6:

Ingredients
1 3/4 oz (50g) bulgur *← Quinoa*
2 tomatoes
1 red onion
1 bunch parsley
1 bunch mint
Juice of 1 lemon
2 tbsp olive oil
Ground cumin
Salt

Cooking instructions
1. Boil Half a glass of water. Soak bulgur wheat in the hot water and let it rise. Add the olive oil, lemon juice, salt and 1/2 teaspoon of cumin. Leave to cool.
2. Wash And trim the herbs. Dry and chop coarsely. Add to the cold tabbouleh and mix well.

You can also add tomatoes, seeded and cut into small pieces, and finely chopped onion as well. Keep cool until ready to serve.

Roasted winter vegetable and millet salad
Total time: 40 mins
Serves: 2

Ingredients
3-4 cups of assorted brussels sprouts, carrots, butternut squash, and sweet potatoes
1 tablespoon olive oil
1 small red onion
1 cup cooked millet, cooled
2-3 handfuls spinach or kale

Dressing:
1 clove garlic, minced
2 tablespoon olive oil
2 tablespoons good balsamic vinegar
Pinch of salt and pepper
Hummus to serve

Instructions
Preheat oven to 400°.
Cut veggies into 1/4"-1/2" size pieces. Toss with 1 tablespoon olive oil and roast for 25-35 minutes until all are tender and browning. Remove from oven.
In a large bowl combine millet, spinach, and roasted veggies.
Whisk together 2 tablespoons olive oil, 2 tablespoons vinegar, minced garlic, salt, and pepper. Pour over salad and toss well.
Serve with a side of hummus if desired.

Pomegranate-bulgur salad
quinoa

Ingredients
1 cup bulgur ← *quinoa sub*
1 teaspoon kosher salt

1 cup boiling water
4 scallions, thinly sliced on the bias
1/2 cup parsley leaves, chopped
1/2 cup mint leaves, chopped
1/3 cup golden raisins
1 cup pomegranate seeds
2 tablespoons fresh lemon juice
2 tablespoons extra-virgin olive oil
Freshly ground black pepper

Directions
In a medium bowl, combine bulgur and salt. Top with boiling water and cover bowl with a plate until water is absorbed, 30 minutes.
Toss with scallions, parsley, mint, raisins, pomegranate seeds, lemon juice, and olive oil, and season to taste with salt and pepper.

Protein packed plant-based meatballs

Ingredients
1 cup dry lentils (180g)
1/2 cup dry millet (95g)
1 cup yellow onion (130g)
1 cup walnuts (90g)
1/4 cup tomato paste (60g)
1 cup fresh parsley (20g)
5 garlic cloves, minced
1 teaspoon dried oregano
1 teaspoon dried basil
2 teaspoons salt (12g)
1/2 cup water (120ml)
1/4 cup rice flour (40g)

Directions

Cook lentils by bringing 4 cups of water (945ml) to a boil.
Add 1 cup of lentils, turn heat to low and simmer for 50 minutes until lentils are cooked, stirring occasionally.
Place cooked lentils in a large mixing bowl.
Cook millet by placing 1 cup of water (250ml) and 1/2 cup of millet in a pot.
Bring to a simmer, turn to low and cook for 20 minutes, stirring occasionally.
Place cooked millet in the mixing bowl with the lentils.
Add the remaining ingredients, except for the rice flour to the mixing bowl (onion, walnuts, tomato paste, parsley,garlic, oregano, basil, salt and water).
Stir mixture so that all of the ingredients are combined.
Place the mixture in a food processor and process until smooth (you may have to do this in two batches depending on the size of your food processor).
Once all of the meatball mixture has been processed, place it back in the large bowl and sprinkle in the rice flour.
Stir until the rice flour is mixed in.
Preheat oven to 350°.
Take the mixture and roll into whatever size meatballs you like. (if you make them about the size in the picture, you will get around 25 meatballs)
Place them on a very lightly greased baking sheet and bake for 35 minutes.

Gingered millet with japanese veggies

Ingredients
Gingered millet with japanese veggies
1 cup - millet
1 (15 ounce) - black beans
2 -3 tablespoons - fresh ginger

1/4 teaspoon - sea salt
3 cups - water
1 cup - shiitake mushroom
2 medium - carrots
1 small - bok choy
1/2 cup - red cabbage
3 - scallions
2 tablespoons - sunflower seeds
3 tablespoons - sesame oil
3 tablespoons - apple cider vinegar

Directions
Place millet and ginger in a small saucepan. Add 1/2 teaspoon salt
and water. Bring to a boil, stir once, then reduce heat and simmer,
covered, for 25 minutes. Allow to rest for 10 minutes, then fluff
with a fork, add beans.
• steam shiitakes in a steamer over boiling water, covered, for 3
minutes. Add carrots and bok choy and steam 4 to 6 minutes
more. Remove steamer from heat.
• in a small bowl, whisk together oil and vinegar to make
dressing. Season with a dash of salt.
• transfer millet to bowls and garnish with steamed and remaining
raw vegetables. Season to taste with salt and pepper. Pour
dressing over top and sprinkle with sunflower seeds

Matcha chia pudding with sweet dukkah
Total time-8 hours 30 mins
Yield: 2-4 servings

Ingredients
1¼ cups unsweetened almond milk
1 tbsp matcha powder
4 tsp honey ← light or dark corn syrup, maple syrup
3 tbsp chia seeds

¼ cup toasted whole almonds
2 tbsp toasted sesame seeds
2 tbsp cacao nibs
2 tsp coconut sugar
Pinch of salt

Instructions
Whisk together the almond milk and matcha powder until there
are no lumps. Next whisk in the honey until combined, and then
the chia seeds. Cover with plastic wrap and store in the fridge
overnight or for 6-8 hours. Add more liquid in the morning if
needed.
In a small food processor, process the almonds until broken up
into small pebble-sized pieces. Then add the sesame seeds, cacao
nibs, coconut sugar, and salt, pulse one or two times until
combined.
Divide the matcha chia pudding into bowls and top with the
dukkah. Drizzle honey on top if desired.

Quinoa Bulgur vegetable chili

Ingredients
1 green pepper
1 onion
3 cloves garlic
1 zucchini
1 carrot
1 1/2 cups corn (i used frozen)
8 oz. cherry tomatoes
15 oz. can kidney beans, rinsed and drained
2/3 cup bulgur (or 1/2 cup for less thick) ← quinoa
15 oz. can tomato sauce (1 1/2 cups)
3 cups vegetable broth
1 tsp. cumin

1 tsp. chili powder
1/2 tsp. paprika
1/4 tsp. cayenne pepper (more for a bigger kick)

Directions
prep veggies: dice onion, bell pepper, carrot, zucchini, mince garlic, and halve tomatoes.
In a stockpot over medium-high heat, sauté onion, bell pepper, carrot, zucchini, and garlic for about 7-8 minutes.
Add corn, tomatoes, and spices. Sauté another 3 minutes.
Add 3 cups broth, tomato sauce, bulgur, and beans. Bring to a boil, then reduce heat and let simmer for 15 minutes, stirring occasionally, until bulgur is cooked. (or about 45 minutes if using regular bulgur.)
It will become very thick as the bulgur absorbs the liquid, and even more after sitting a bit. Add more broth/water to thin it out if desired.

Lunch of millet, black beans, avocado and smoky paprika tahini

Ingredients
Cooked millet
Black beans
Avocado
Toasted pumpkin seeds
Sliced red radishes
Fresh parsley or cilantro

Method
Add all the above and top with dressing - recipe below

Smoky tahini dressing
Serves 1-2
2 tbsp creamy tahini
2 tsp tamari – soy sauce G-F
2 tsp fresh lemon juice
1 tbsp water
1 tsp pure maple syrup
¼ heaping tsp smoked paprika

Method for tahini
Add to a bowl and combine until creamy

15 minute brussels sprout & tempeh stir-fry

Ingredients
(20) brussels sprouts, washed, trimmed & halved
(1#) plain tempeh, cubed
(4) green onions, chopped & divided between greens & whites
(3) garlic cloves (optional – i omitted these)
(2) tbsp grated fresh ginger
(2) medium carrots, peeled & sliced on the diagonal
(1) medium red bell pepper, seeded and chopped fine
(1) tbsp cornstarch
(3) tbsp soy sauce
(2) tbsp rice vinegar (seasoned or unseasoned)
(1/4) cup water
(4) tbsp sesame oil, for the stir-frying

Directions
Start by combining the cornstarch, soy sauce, rice vinegar & water in a small bowl with a whisk. Mix and set aside.
As with any stir-fry or curry dish, the most important thing is be prepared with all of the ingredients before cooking. Prepare & cut

the brussels and set aside in a separate bowl. Prepare the tempeh and set aside in a separate bowl. Finally, prepare the green onions (setting aside the greens separately in a bowl on their own) and the ginger & optional garlic. Prep the carrots & bell pepper and set them aside together.

When ready to cook, heat a large cast iron frying pan or a wok on high and add 2 tbsp of sesame oil. Once hot, add the brussels sprout halves and cook, tossing here and there to prevent burning, for 4 minutes. Set the brussels sprouts aside in a medium bowl. Give the pan a little wipe with a paper towel and return the pan to the stove.

Heating another tbsp of sesame oil, this time add the cubed tempeh and cook in the oil (you may need to add a little more oil). Cook, stirring, for 4-5 minutes until the cubes are golden, starting to brown, and a little (deliciously) crispy.

Set the tempeh aside with the brussels sprouts (you can use the same bowl). Wipe the pan again and return it to the stove.

Next, heat the remaining tbsp of sesame oil, and cook the ginger, green onions & garlic (if using) for one minute, until fragrant, being careful not to burn the garlic. Next, add the green onion whites, carrots, & red pepper. Stir frequently and cook for 2 minutes until the colors are bright and they are just softened. Keeping the heat on, add the cooked sprouts & the tempeh to the pan and mix all of the vegetables well together. To finish, give the bowl of prepared sauce a good stir with the whisk and pour the entire lot over the hot vegetables. Stir well as it thickens from the cornstarch. Cook, stirring constantly, for a final 2-3 minutes until glossy, hot & gorgeous.

Serve on its own, or with cooked rice, garnished with the sliced green onions. On its own, this meal makes for a rather satisfying plate, though those with appetites for more may wish to include some grains.

As i mentioned earlier, this dish keeps incredibly well in the fridge for days and re-heats so well you may even find you like it better as the week goes by. It's hearty & filling while still being 100% plant-based. A super powered meal if i ever saw one.

General tso's tempeh

Total time-20 mins
Serves: 3-4

Ingredients
Tempeh
1-2 8 ounce packages of tempeh (organic is best)
¼ cup cornstarch (preferably non-gmo)
½ tsp garlic powder
½ tsp paprika
1 tb avocado or olive oil
General tso's sauce
Avocado or olive oil (drizzle for the pan)
2 tsp ginger, minced
2 cloves of garlic, minced
½ cup vegetable broth
2 tb tamari sauce (or soy sauce if not gluten free)
2 tb tomato paste
1 tb rice vinegar
1 tb vegan hoisin sauce
2 tsp maple syrup

Instructions
Tempeh prep
Preheat a steaming pan.
Cut the tempeh package into half or thirds.
Steam the tempeh chunks for 10 minutes. Remove from heat, cut
the tempeh into bite size chunks. (you can stop here if you prefer
not to fry your tempeh and skip to the sauce prep instructions).
Mix the cornstarch, garlic powder, and paprika and pour into a
plastic bag.
Lightly coat each piece of tempeh with the cornstarch mixture,
shaking off any excess.

Preheat a skillet on medium heat.
When hot, coat the bottom of the pan with oil.
Add the tempeh pieces.
Cook the tempeh until golden brown.
When crispy, remove from pan.
Sauce prep
Using the same pan, and add a drizzle more oil and toss in the
fresh garlic and ginger.
After a few minutes, mix veggie broth, soy sauce, rice vinegar,
tomato paste, hoisin sauce, and maple syrup in the pan with the
garlic and ginger.
Add the tempeh and stir to coat each piece with sauce.
Turn down the heat and saute for 5 minutes until the sauce
thickens.

Roasted root vegetable salad with millet
Cook time: 1 hour
serves 4

Ingredients
1 cup raw millet
2 cups of water/broth
1 tbsp of salt
3 cups root vegetables of your choice – peeled, diced (sweet
potato, carrot, golden beet, purple potato, celery root, parsnip,
rutabaga, turnip, yam)
1/2 cup cilantro leaves, chopped ← parsley
1 cup dill/mint/basil leaves, chopped
5 radish – sliced
1 pomegranate seeds
salt & pepper

Directions
Preheat the oven to 350°f.

Wash, peel and cut the root vegetables in small cubes. Mix vegetables with olive oil and season with salt and pepper. Place them on parchment paper lined baking sheet without over crowding. Roast them for 15- 20 minutes until cooked through and lightly caramelized.

Heat a large saucepan on medium heat. Toast the raw millet for 5 minutes until fragrant and start making popping sound. Add 2 cups of water in the saucepan carefully and season with salt. Give a good stir. Turn the heat to high and bring the mixture to a boil. Lower the heat, cover the pot and simmer for about 15 minutes until all the liquid get absorbed. Removed from the heat and let sit for 10 minutes. Now, fluff cooked millet with fork, and taste for seasoning.

Add roasted vegetables, chopped herbs, slices of radishes and pomegranate seeds to the cooked millet. Add cilantro lemon dressing and mix well. Serve hot or cold!

Cilantro lemon dressing
1/2 cup cilantro leaves
2 lemon juice
3 tbsp extra virgin olive oil
1 tbsp honey – optional
salt & pepper

Put all the ingredients in food processor and blend until smooth consistency. Taste for seasoning.

Vegan asian orange tempeh
Total time-2 hours 30 mins
Serves: 2

Ingredients
4 oz soba noodles
8 oz tempeh
Orange sauce:
½ cup vegetable broth
¼ cup orange juice

3 tbsp maple syrup
2 tbsp rice vinegar
2 tbsp soy sauce
2 cloves garlic, minced
4 tsp arrowroot powder or cornstarch + 2 tbsp water
2 tsp orange zest
1 tsp sriracha
½ tsp pepper
½ tsp ground ginger
½ tsp celery salt
Optional garnish: green onions & sesame seeds

Instructions
In a medium bowl combine all the sauce ingredients except the arrow root powder and whisk together well.
Cut the tempeh into 20-24 small pieces, about equal size, and place them into the sauce. Place that in the fridge to marinate for about 2 hours. Feel free to marinate the tempeh even longer if you'd like! After you're done marinating - continue to the next steps.
Bring a pot of water to a boil.
This next part requires some multitasking, so read through the recipe first:
Place the soba noodles in a pot of boiling water too cook.
At the same time, place the sauce without the tempeh into a small sauce pan (reserving ¼ cup for the next step), and mix the arrowroot dissolved in water. Cook on medium heat for 4-5 minutes, until thickened.
While you are cooking the noodles and making the sauce, take ¼ cup of the marinade, toss with the marinaded tempeh - cook for about 4-7 minutes until nice and hot!
Drain the soba noodles and run under cool water to stop the cooking.
Per serving, layer ½ the noodles onto a dish then add ½ of the cooked tempeh, and top with your desired amount of orange sauce
Optional: garnish with green onions and sesame seeds - this

makes the pictures pretty!
Sit back, relax, and enjoy!

Mediterranean-inspired vegetables over millet

Ingredients
1 cup uncooked millet
Vegetable broth, optional
2 tablespoons extra virgin olive oil
½ medium onion, chopped
1 zucchini, cut in half lengthwise then sliced
½ eggplant, chopped
2 very ripe medium tomatoes
3 cloves of garlic, chopped
1 tablespoon tomato paste
1 teaspoon cumin
1 teaspoon smoked paprika
Pinch of cayenne pepper
Pinch of salt
Cracked black pepper
Pitted kalamata olives, chopped (approximately 8-10)
Juice of ½ of one lemon

Directions
1. Rinse millet and combine with 2 cups of water (or broth) in a medium saucepan. Bring to a boil, cover, reduce heat to low and simmer for 15 minutes. Take a quick peek to make sure all of the liquid has been absorbed. When it is, remove from heat and keep covered for 10 minutes. Fluff with a fork.
2. In a large sauté pan, heat olive oil over medium heat. Add the onion and sauté for about 3 minutes. Stir in the zucchini, eggplant, tomatoes and garlic, stirring constantly (to prevent the garlic from burning) for another minute.
3. Add the tomato paste, cumin, smoked paprika, cayenne, salt

and pepper. Add a splash or two of water to prevent sticking if necessary. Cover the pan and cook for 10-15 minutes, stirring every 5 minutes until the flavors have melded and vegetables are to your desired tenderness.

4. Remove from heat and adjust seasoning to your liking. Squeeze in the lemon juice, toss in the olives and stir well.

5. Serve over the millet and enjoy!

Coconut curried skillet farro and chickpeas with smoky potatoes

Total time: 30 mins

Ingredients
Farro:
3 1/2 cups cooked farro
1 1/2 tbsp vegan butter
1 1/2 tbsp curry powder
1/4 tsp cinnamon
1/4 cup flat leaf parsley, finely chopped
1 1/2 cups kale, chopped and packed (or try frozen kale)
16oz canned chickpeas, drained and rinsed
1/4 cup coconut milk (or coconut cream)
1/4 cup chopped raw almonds
2 tsp maple syrup, grade b
Optional: pinch of fresh orange peel or golden raisins (optional)
Potatoes:
1 1/2 cups potato, peeled and diced (any variety)
1 tsp smoked paprika
1 tbsp virgin coconut oil
Whole dish: salt and pepper to taste (i added about 1/3 tsp pink salt)

Directions

Precook your farro, since this will take a good hour to get your farro tender you may want to do this part the day before like i did, so when you are ready for dinner, you can whip up this dish in under thirty minutes, easy! Cook farro by boiling it in a large pot of water until all the water has absorbed and farro has bloomed and is tender. I usually slowly simmer my farro in water for at least 60 minutes. Drain any excess water and place cooked farro in the fridge to chill.

To prepare farro: warm a skillet over high heat and melt the vegan butter. Add the cooked farro, curry and cinnamon and sautè over high for about two minutes.

To the farro, add in the chickpeas and coconut milk, optional citrus ingredient and fold. Fold and sautè for another few miutes until the coconut milk has absorbed. Then push all the farro mixture over to one side of the pan leaving a blank space.

Add the chopped almonds to the blank spot and drizzle the maple over top them. Stir the maple almonds for a minute, then fold them into the rest of the mixture.

Reduce heat to low and fold in the kale and parsley and optional orange zest.

While the farro mixture is on low heat, bring a small pot of water to a boil and boil the potatoes for 4-6 minutes or until tender but not mushy. Drain potatoes and set aside.

Transfer the farro mixture to your serving bowl, and in the same skillet, turn up stove heat to high and melt the coconut oil into the skillet. Add the potatoes, paprika and salt and pepper. Saute potatoes 3-4 minutes, or until edges brown and crisp up. Pour potatoes on the side of the farro in the serving dish to serve. Serve warm. Delicious warm or chilled.

Mexican tempeh quinoa salad
Yield-4 to 6 servings
Cook time -45 mins

Ingredients
1 cup quinoa
2 cups water
1 tablespoon olive oil
1/2 onion, chopped
1 red pepper, diced
1 (8-oz.) package tempeh, diced into bite-size pieces
1 cup salsa
juice from one lime
1 teaspoon cumin
1/4 teaspoon cayenne pepper
1/4 teaspoon salt
1/4 teaspoon pepper
1 (15-oz.) can black beans, drained and rinsed
1 cup fresh corn (or frozen)
1/2 cup cherry tomatoes, halved
2 tablespoons fresh cilantro
salt and pepper, to taste
1 avocado, diced

Directions
Place the quinoa and water in a covered pot on high heat. Once it starts to boil, reduce to simmer and cook for 20 minutes or until the water is absorbed and the quinoa is fluffy.
While the quinoa is cooking, prepare the tempeh. Heat the oil in a pan on medium heat, and add the chopped onion. Cook for 5 minutes.
Add the diced red pepper, tempeh, salsa, lime juice, cumin, cayenne pepper, and salt and pepper.
Cook the tempeh mixture, stirring occasionally, for about 15 minutes.
Once the quinoa and tempeh are cooked, pour both into a glass bowl and mix together. Add the beans, corn, tomatoes, cilantro, and a little salt and pepper, and mix well. Serve and top with a few pieces of diced avocado.
Enjoy as is, or use as a delicious filling for burritos.
Nutrition

Peanut butter basil tempeh with broccoli
Total time-25 mins
Serves: 2-3

Ingredients
For the peanut sauce
2 tbsp. natural peanut butter
2 tbsp. water
1 tbsp. soy sauce or tamari
1 tbsp. maple syrup or agave
1 tbsp. lime juice
½ tbsp. fresh grated ginger
For the tempeh
2 tbsp. lime juice
1 tbsp. soy sauce or tamari
1 tsp. fresh grated ginger
1 garlic clove, minced
1-8 oz. package of tempeh, diced into ½ inch cubes
1 tbsp. vegetable oil
For the broccoli stir fry
1 tbsp. vegetable oil
1 garlic clove, minced
1 medium broccoli crown, chopped into florets
¼ cup fresh basil leaves, packed
Cooked rice, for serving

Instructions
Make the peanut sauce
Whisk all ingredients together in a small bowl.
Make the tempeh
Whisk together lime juice, soy sauce or tamari, ginger and garlic
in a small bowl. Add tempeh cubes and toss to coat. Optionally

marinade for 30 minutes.

Coat the bottom of a medium skillet with oil and place over medium heat. Add tempeh cubes, reserving marinade. Cook about 4 minutes, until browned on bottoms. Flip and cook another 4 minutes. Add marinade to skillet and continue cooking until liquid has cooked off, about 1 minute more. Transfer tempeh to a plate.

Make the broccoli stir fry

Add oil to skillet and raise heat to high. Add garlic and broccoli. Stir-fry until broccoli is tender-crisp, about 3 minutes. Add peanut sauce and cook about 1 minute more, just until heated through and ingredients are incorporated. Add a few tablespoons of water if skillet becomes too dry. Remove from heat and stir in basil. Serve over rice.

Oriental bulgur-lentil-salad

For 2 servings

Ingredients
For the salad
100 g bulgur
80 g red lentils
200 ml vegetable stock
2 shallots
1 clove of garlic
1 big red chili peppers
5 tbsp argan oil
1/2 cucumber
80 g pistachios
1 handful of mint
Juice and some zest of a organic lime
Spice mix as required
Sea salt
Black pepper
For the spice mix

1 tsp fenugreek seeds
1 tsp dried sweet red peppers
1/2 tsp coriander seeds
1 tsp cumin seeds
5 cinnamon flowers
2 pods green cardamom
1 tsp coconut sugar

Directions

Prepare bulgur according to the directions on the package but replace the hot water with boiling vegetable stock. Cook the red lentils 10–15 minutes in the double amount of water and season with salt when they are almost done. During cooking the lentils and bulgur, grain the ingredients for the spice mix to powder. Halve the chili pepper, remove the seeds and chop it as well as the garlic and the shallots and sweat everything in a pan. Add the spice mix and deglaze with lime juice, then add the lentils and the bulgur, season with salt and pepper and let it cool down in a bowl. Husk the pistachios and chop them as well as the mint leaves and dice the cucumber. Add to the cold mass with 4 tablespoons argan oil and mix it well. At least, season with some lime zest, salt and pepper. If necessary, add some vegetable stock and let it soak for some minutes. It gets more flavor if you let it soak over night.

Balsamic roasted brussels sprouts with polenta

Total time:40 mins
Serves: 2 servings

Ingredients
1 cup water
1 cup low-sodium vegetable broth
½ cup medium-grind polenta
1 tablespoon butter
Salt and pepper, to taste

½ pound brussels sprouts
1/4 medium red onion, thinly sliced
2 teaspoons olive oil
Pinch of salt
Pinch of black pepper
½ cup balsamic vinegar
2 tablespoons chopped toasted walnut pieces

Instructions
Bring the vegetable broth and water to a boil in a medium pot.
Add in the polenta, whisking quite a bit, until the mixture begins
to thicken. Reduce the heat to a simmer, cover, and let cook for
25 to 30 minutes, stirring every once in awhile (full technique can
be found here- it's the only way i make polenta). Once done, stir
in butter and salt/pepper as desired.
Preheat oven to 400°. Trim the ends from the brussels sprouts and
cut each brussels sprout in half, keeping any leaves that fall off.
Toss the brussels sprouts, loose leaves, and onions with olive oil,
salt and pepper. Spread out into a single layer on a roasting pan
and bake for 15 to 20 minutes, stirring once halfway through.
Brussels sprouts should be browning.
While the brussels sprouts are roasting, place the balsamic
vinegar in a small sauce pan. Bring to a boil, reduce heat to
medium-low, and let cook until mixture has reduced down to 1/4
cup and has thickened slightly, 8 to 10 minutes.
Once brussels sprouts are finished, toss with 1 to 2 tablespoons of
the balsamic mixture and walnut pieces.
Divide polenta into two bowls and top with brussels sprout
mixture.

Tempeh cauliflower butternut in teriyaki sauce

Total time-45 mins

Serves: 2

Ingredients

Teriyaki sauce

9 large medjool dates soaked in hot water for 15 minutes

¼ cup low sodium soy sauce

¾ cup water or veggie broth

2 tsp or more rice vinegar

1 tsp molasses

½ tsp garlic powder

¼ tsp onion powder

¼ tsp or more cayenne

1 tsp or more grated ginger

1 tsp sesame oil

1 tbsp or more maple or coconut sugar if needed

For the veggies:

8 oz tempeh, cubed and steamed, or use tofu

½ head of a small cauliflower chopped into small florets, or use broccoli

1 loaded cup chopped butternut squash or other squash

Toasted sesame seeds for garnish

Instructions

Soak the dates if you haven't. Steam the tempeh for 10 minutes or boil for 10 minutes. Drain and keep aside.

Preheat the oven to 425 degrees f. Chop up the squash and cauliflower. Spray oil on the veggies, place on parchment and bake at 425 degrees f for 15 to 20 minutes or al dente. Or you can steam the veggies, or boil with the tempeh until just about done. Drain the dates and blend with the other sauce ingredients until smooth. Pour the sauce into a skillet over medium heat. Add tempeh, roasted cauliflower and butternut squash. Cover and cook for 4 to 5 minutes, or until the sauce comes to a good boil. Carefully taste and adjust sweet and salt in the sauce. If the sauce is not sweet enough, add maple or coconut sugar or other sweetener. Continue to simmer over low heat for a few minutes or until the vegetables are done to preference and the sauce has thickened. Take off heat and let it sit for 5 minutes before serving.

The sauce will continue to thicken as it cools.
Serve over rice/ grains of choice with a garnish of toasted sesame seeds and green onions.

Butternut, barley & lentil pilaf
sorghum

Yield: 4 servings as a main, 6-8 as a side

Ingredients
Pilaf: *sorghum*
1/2 c pearl barley (for gf use brown/wild rice or another hearty gf grain)
1/2 c puy lentils
Small butternut squash (approx 680g/1 1/2lb), peeled and cubed
1 tbsp olive oil
1/2 tsp ground cumin
1/2 tsp ground coriander
1/4 tsp cinnamon
1/4 tsp garlic powder
Large pinch of salt
1/3 c raisins
1/3 c pumpkin seeds, toasted (reserve 1-2 tbsp for topping)
1/3 c finely chopped red onion
1/2 c roughly chopped parsley

Dressing:
3 tbsp orange juice (fresh)
1 tbsp red wine vinegar
1 tbsp extra-virgin olive oil
Salt + pepper (to taste)

Instructions
Preheat oven to 200c/400f
Cook lentils & barley in two separate pots according to package instructions. Barley typically takes 40-45 minutes and puy lentils

approx 25 minutes. When al dente, drain and set aside.

In a large mixing bowl, combine cubed squash with olive oil, spices and a large pinch of salt. Spread in a layer on a baking sheet and roast for approx 25 minutes, or until soft when pierced with a fork.

Meanwhile, whisk together the dressing ingredients and add to barley and lentils along with the raisins, pumpkin seeds and red onion. Toss well.

Finally, fold through the roasted butternut and the parsley, transfer to a serving dish and scatter the remaining pumpkin seeds on top.

Sesame kale glow bowl
Serves 3

Ingredients
1 cup quinoa
1 tablespoon coconut oil/sesame oil
1/2 of a red onion
1 clove garlic, minced
3 cups kale, de-stemmed + torn
2 cups broccoli florets (about 1 small head)
4 ounces of tempeh, chopped/crumbled
2 tablespoons tamari/soy sauce
2 tablespoons water
Juice from 1/2 - 1 lime, depending on your liking
1/2 tablespoon dijon mustard
1 teaspoon fresh ginger, minced (or powdered)
1/2 teaspoon black pepper
Dash of red pepper flakes (optional)
2 tablespoons sesame seeds (black or white)

Instructions
Combine 1 cup quinoa with 2 cups water in a medium-sized pot.

Bring to a boil and reduce heat to simmer for about 15 minutes or until all water has been absorbed.

Meanwhile, in a small saucepan, melt the coconut oil on medium-high heat. Add the red onion and sauté for 2-3 minutes. Add the garlic, kale, broccoli and tempeh. Sauté for about 3 minutes.

In a small bowl, combine the tamari, water, lime juice, dijon mustard, ginger, pepper, red pepper flakes and sesame seeds. Add mixture to saucepan with vegetables and mix until well combined. Cook for about 2 more minutes.

Once quinoa is finished cooking, scoop it into 2-3 bowls and top with the vegetable mixture. Add extra tamari/soy sauce as needed. Enjoy!

Three bean ~~barley~~ buckwheat chili

Yield: serves 4 to 6
Cook time: 35 minutes

Ingredients
2 cups cooked beans (i used a mix of pinto beans, speckled butter beans, and black eyed peas)
1/3 cup barley ← buckwheat
2 stalks celery, diced
1 medium onion, diced
2 carrots, diced
1 parsnip, diced (optional)
1 can petite diced tomatoes
1 heaping tbsp tomato paste
2 tbsp vegan bbq sauce (see this recipe)
3-4 cups vegetable broth or water, plus more to cover the bottom of the pan - here's an easy way to make veggie broth at home

Seasonings:
1 dried smoked chipotle pepper
1 tbsp cumin
1/2 tbsp chili powder

1/2 tbsp paprika
Salt, pepper to taste

Instructions
Heat a big saucepan over medium heat. Add a couple tbsp of vegetable broth or water to the bottom of the pan. When the broth/water start bubbling, add onions, celery, carrots, and parsnip. Sautee for 5-7 min until the vegetables are soft, adding more broth/water if necessary.

In a separate saucepan, bring the rest of the broth/water to a boil. Add the rest of the ingredients (except for salt and pepper) to the big pot with the celery-carrot mix. Stir well, cover with the boiling broth/water until the vegetables are just covered.

Let simmer for 25-35 min, adding more broth/water if the chili starts getting too thick. Add salt and pepper towards the end.

Fish out the chipotle pepper and discard if you prefer a milder chili. If you like it spicy, cut off 1/2 of the chipotle and mash really well, then add back to the pot. Want it fiery spicy? Mash up and use the whole thing!

Scrambled tempeh with watercress

Ingredients
1 pack of tempeh
2 cups of watercress/kale/spinach
1 tablespoon of tamari soy sauce
2 tablespoon of coconut oil
1 tablespoon of hemp seed oil
½ cup of slice onion
1 garlic cloves
2 tablespoon of ground turmeric
¼ cup of vegetable broth
Salt/pepper according to your taste
½ tablespoon of curry powder

Instructions
Heat the coconut oil in a frying pan.
Add onion and garlic, cook until they turn yellow and add broken tempeh.
Cook for about 2 minutes and add vegetable broth, turmeric, curry powder.
Cook for another 2 minutes before you add watercress/kale/spinach
Cook for one minute and drizzle with hemp oil (you can skip this one if you like)
And you're done

Roasted butternut squash carrot barley farro sorghum quinoa salad

buckwheat groats
brown rice

Serves: ~ 18 cups

Ingredients
Roasted butternut squash and carrots
4 cups butternut squash, but into ½" cubes
2 cups carrots, cut into ½' pieces (i used rainbow carrots for more color)
3 tablespoons olive oil, divided
1 tablespoon chopped fresh sage leaves
1 tablespoon chopped fresh thyme leaves
Salt and fresh ground pepper, to taste
Stewed figs and cranberries
1 cup dried figs
¼ cup dried cranberries
2 cups apple cider
Grain salad
4 cups cooked barley ← _buckwheat groats_
2 cups cooked farro ← _brown rice_
2 cups cooked quinoa
2 cups cooked whole sorghum
3 tablespoons extra virgin olive oil

2 tablespoons pomegranate balsamic vinegar
¾ cup parsley, minced
1 teaspoon fresh thyme leaves
1½ cups pomegranate seeds
Juice from one clementine
Salt and fresh ground pepper, to taste

Directions
Roasted butternut squash and carrots
Preheat oven to 400 degrees. In a large bowl, toss together butternut squash, 2 tablespoons olive oil, sage, thyme, salt and pepper. Spread in a single layer on a baking sheet. Place carrots, remaining tablespoon olive oil, salt and pepper in the bowl; toss together, then spread in a single layer on another baking sheet. Place both baking sheets in the oven. Roast carrots about 20 minutes, until tender; roast butternut squash 20-25 minutes until tender.
Stewed figs and cranberries
Place figs, cranberries and apple cider in a saucepan; bring to a boil, then reduce heat to low and simmer, covered, for 15 minutes; turn off heat and let sit until you are ready to assemble the salad. When ready to use, remove figs from reduced apple cider and cut off stems; cut figs into quarters. Reserve reduced apple cider and cranberries.
Grain salad
Place cooked grains in a large serving bowl and toss with olive oil, vinegar, parsley, thyme, pomegranate seeds, clementine juice, roasted butternut squash and carrots, figs, reduced apple cider and cranberries. Season to taste with salt and pepper.

Quinoa and cauliflower salad with popped sorghum
Total time: 50 min
Servings: 4

Ingredients
1 cup small (1-inch) cauliflower florets
5 tablespoons extra-virgin olive oil
Kosher salt
1/2 cup red quinoa, rinsed
1/2 cup white quinoa, rinsed
1/4 cup vegetable oil, if popping sorghum
1/4 cup popping sorghum, or 2 cups popped sorghum (see note)
1 tablespoon minced chives
1 teaspoon unseasoned rice vinegar

Preheat the oven to 350°. On a rimmed baking sheet, drizzle the cauliflower with 1 tablespoon of the olive oil, season with salt and toss to coat. Roast for about 15 minutes, stirring occasionally, until tender and golden brown. Let cool.

Meanwhile, bring 2 medium saucepans of lightly salted water to a simmer. Cook the red quinoa and white quinoa separately over moderate heat until tender, 12 to 15 minutes. Drain and rinse under cold running water. Drain well.

If popping sorghum, heat the vegetable oil in a medium, heavy pot until almost smoking. Add the sorghum, cover and cook over moderately high heat, shaking the pot occasionally, until the popping has almost stopped; pour into a bowl and season with salt.

In a large bowl, combine the cauliflower, red and white quinoa, almonds, chives, rice vinegar and the remaining 1/4 cup of olive oil. Season with salt and toss well. Transfer the salad to plates, top with the popped sorghum and serve

Barley risotto with fava beans and mushrooms
Serves 4

Ingredients
1 ½ to 1 ¾ pounds fresh fava beans

3 medium ears very fresh, tender sweet corn
3 tablespoons extra virgin olive oil, divided
2 cloves garlic, minced
½ cup finely chopped sweet onion, such as vidalia
1 ½ cups pearled barley
½ cup dry white wine
4 cups vegetable stock, plus more if needed
Salt to taste
½ pound oyster mushrooms, trimmed and sliced
2 teaspoons lemon juice
2 tablespoons chopped flat-leaf parsley
2 tablespoons chopped fresh basil
Freshly ground black pepper

Preparation
Remove the beans from their pods. Bring a pot of water to boil, and blanch the favas for 1 minute. Drain and immediately plunge into ice water. Skin the fava beans (open a section of the skin and pop the beans out). You should have about ¾ cup.
Cut the kernels off the corn. You should have about 1½ cups.
Place half the corn and about a third of the fava beans in a food processor and process until very smooth.
Heat half the oil over medium heat in a skillet. Add the mushrooms and sauté for 5 minutes. Set aside.
Heat the remaining oil over medium heat in a large deep saucepan or a dutch oven. Add the onion and garlic and cook for 3-4 minutes, stirring frequently. Add the barley. Cook, stirring, for 1-2 minutes.
Add the wine. Cook for a minute or two, until the wine has mostly evaporated.
Add a half cup of broth. Cook, stirring nearly constantly, until the broth is absorbed. Repeat the process, adding the broth in half-cup increments. Continue until the barley is al dente, about 30-35 minutes. You should have used about 3 cups of broth, although some barley will require more. Add salt to taste, depending on the saltiness of your vegetable broth.
Add the fava beans, corn, mushrooms, lemon juice and fava-corn

puree. Stir in the final cup of broth, and cook another 5 minutes, stirring gently a few times. Stir in the parsley, basil and black pepper, and serve.

Tropical chia coconut-mango granola
Active: 10 min
Total time: 40 min
Servings: 5 cups

Ingredients
3 cups old-fashioned rolled oats
1/4 cup chia seeds
1 cup shredded unsweetened coconut
3/4 teaspoon flaky sea salt
1/4 cup plus 2 tablespoons honey
3 tablespoons coconut oil
1/2 teaspoon vanilla extract
1 tablespoon grated lemon zest
1 cup dried mango, diced into 1/4-inch pieces

How to make this recipe
Preheat the oven to 325°. Line one large baking sheet with parchment paper.
In a small saucepan over low heat, stir the oil and honey together just until it begins to simmer. Remove from heat and stir in the vanilla extract and lemon zest.
In a mixing bowl combine the oats, chia seeds, shredded coconut and sea salt. Pour the warm honey mixture over the dry ingredients and stir very well to coat. Spread into an even layer on the lined pan. Bake for 10 minutes; remove from the oven and stir every 5 minutes or so until the granola is an even light golden brown on all sides, about 20-25 minutes.
While the granola is still hot, mix in the chopped mango pieces until they are evenly distributed. The granola will crisp up on the

baking sheet as it cools.

Simple sorghum arugula salad with gluten-free rye croutons
total time-1 hour 10 mins
Serves: 4

Ingredients
1 cup sorghum
3 cups water

Gluten-free rye croutons
4 slices canyon bakehouse gluten-free deli rye style bread, cut into ½ inch cubes
1 tbsp. extra-virgin olive oil
Sea salt and freshly ground pepper, to taste

Salad
2 cups arugula
Handful of finely chopped fresh parsley
Handful of finely chopped fresh basil
4 red radishes, finely diced
½ small red onion, finely diced
2 tbsp. sunflower seeds, optional
Juice of 1 large lemon
1 tbsp. extra-virgin olive oil, plus more if needed for serving
Pinch crushed red pepper flakes
Pinch fresh lemon zest
Sea salt and freshly ground pepper, to taste

Instructions
Cook the sorghum, combine sorghum and water in a medium saucepan and bring to a boil; reduce heat and simmer for 1 hour or until tender. Remove from heat and fluff with a fork.

Preheat oven to 350 degrees f.
Bake cubes of bread on a rimmed baking sheet for 10-12 minutes or until golden brown and crispy. Remove from the oven and set aside.
In a large bowl, combine the arugula, parsley, basil, radishes, red onion, optional sunflower seeds and cooked sorghum. Add the croutons.
In a small bowl, whisk olive oil, crushed red pepper flakes, lemon zest, sea salt and pepper; whisk to combine. Add more oil if needed and drizzle over the arugula mixture. Toss to combine and serve immediately.

Roasted cauliflower & barley bowl
Ingredients for cauliflower bowl

Ingredients
1/2 a head of cauliflower
1 shallot
1/2 a cup of barley
1 handful almond slivers
1 handful raisins
1 small handful parsley
1 teaspoon curry powder
1 teaspoon cinnamon
1 teaspoon salt and pepper
Oil for roasting the vegetables

Directions:
roughly chop the cauliflower and slice the shallot. Toss together with oil, salt and pepper and spices. Roast on baking sheet lined with parchment paper in preheated oven for 10 to 15 minutes on 400f. While the veggies are roasting, cook the barley. Add the raisins to the barley at the last 5 minutes so they moisten and plump up. Assemble everything in a bowl. To finish, drizzle with

good olive oil or walnut oil and a squeeze of of orange juice if you feel like it.

Vegan korean nourish bowl with barley (bibimbap)

Total time-10 mins
serves: 2

Ingredients
1 head of baby bok choy
1 cup of sliced zucchini
½ cup shredded carrots
1 cup cooked chickpeas
¾ cup cooked barley
Kimchi (optional)
Seasoning
1-2 tablespoons gochujang (see note)
1 teaspoon toasted sesame oil
½ teaspoon brown sugar
1-2 teaspoons water

Instructions
Heat 1 teaspoon canola oil in a skillet over medium high heat. Add bok choy and a pinch of salt. Stir-fry for about 3-5 minutes, or until greens are wilted and stalks are crisp-tender. Remove from pan.
In the same skillet, repeat the whole process with carrots and zucchini, cooking for about 2 minutes.
Place in a bowl along with barley, chickpeas and kimchi.
Add the gochujang seasoning and mix thoroughly. Serve immediately.

Crock pot lentils with curry

Prep time: 30 minutes
Cook time: 6 hours
Total time: 6 hours, 30 minutes

Ingredients
3 cups red lentils (masoor dal)*
1 cup finely chopped tomatoes
1/2 cup chopped onion
2-4 fresh green thai, serrano, or cayenne chile peppers stems
removed and finely chopped
1 1/2 tablespoons salt
1 teaspoon ground cumin
1 teaspoon ground coriander
1/2 teaspoon ground turmeric
9 cups water
2 tablespoons vegetable oil
2 teaspoons cumin seeds
1 teaspoon mustard seeds
1 teaspoon ground curry
1/2 cup finely chopped onion
1 (14 oz) can coconut milk
Hot cooked rice

Instructions
Thoroughly wash and rinse lentils, then place in 5-quart slow
cooker with tomatoes, onion, chile peppers, salt, cumin,
coriander, and turmeric.
Stir in the water, cover and cook on low for 5 1/2 hours.
In a large skillet, heat oil over medium high heat.
Add cumin seeds and mustard seeds. Cover and cook until the
mustard seeds pop.
Add curry and chopped onion. Cook and stir until onions are
translucent.
Stir curry mixture and can of coconut milk into slow cooker with
lentils and cook on low for another 30 minutes.
Serve over hot rice.

Sorghum chickpea bowl
Serves: 2-4

Ingredients
1 cup sorghum
1 (15 ounce) bpa-free can chickpeas (garbanzo beans), drained and rinsed
3 tbsp. extra-virgin olive oil
2 tbsp. freshly squeezed lemon juice
1 head kale, stemmed and chopped
1 ripe avocado, peeled, pitted and diced
¼ cup diced white onion
2 roasted red bell pepper slices, finely chopped
½ cup sliced black olives
1 small garlic clove, pressed
2 tbsp. finely chopped fresh basil
2 tbsp. finely chopped fresh parsley
1 scallion, thinly sliced
Sea salt and pepper, to taste

Instructions
Cook sorghum according to package directions.
In a large serving bowl, combine cooked sorghum with remaining ingredients; toss to combine and serve.

Chili-lime popped sorghum
Total time-17 mins
Serves: 4

Ingredients

½ cup uncooked sorghum grain*
2 teaspoons coconut oil
½ cup raw unsalted pepitas
1 cup unsalted pecans
¼ teaspoon chili powder
½ teaspoon ground cumin
½ teaspoon sea salt or to taste
1 teaspoon coconut sugar
2-3 teaspoons fresh lime juice

Instructions
Place an ⅛ cup of the sorghum grain into a paper bag, folding down top. Microwave for 2 to 3 minutes. Transfer popped sorghum and remaining uncooked grains into a medium bowl. Repeat 3 more times for an ⅛ cup at a time. This will ensure you get a higher number of grains to pop.
In a small bowl, combine chili powder, cumin, salt, and coconut sugar.
Place coconut oil in a medium saucepan. Bring to medium heat, and once oil is melted, add pepitas and pecans and toast for 2 to 3 minutes, stirring occasionally. Remove from heat and add the lime juice and half of the spice mixture. Stir to coat.
Pour pepita-pecan mixture into the bowl of popped sorghum. Add remaining spices. Stir to evenly combine and coat. Sprinkle with additional salt as desired.

Sorghum and roasted summer vegetable salad with tarragon and basil
Serves: 4 servings

Ingredients
1 cup dry sorghum
3 cups water
1 large zucchini

1 bunch radishes (about 12 radishes), washed and trimmed
2 ears white or yellow corn, kernels removed (about 1½ - 2 cups kernels)
2 tablespoons olive oil, divided
½ teaspoon dijon mustard
1 tablespoon lemon juice
1 small shallot, chopped
¼ teaspoon salt (plus extra for roasting)
Pepper to taste
¼ cup fresh basil leaves, chopped
¼ cup fresh tarragon leaves, chopped

Instructions
Rinse the sorghum grain in a fine sieve under running water for about a minute. Add it, along with the 3 cups water, to a pot. Bring the grain to a boil and reduce it to a simmer. Simmer for 45-50 minutes, or until the sorghum is tender. Allow the sorghum to cool for 10-15 minutes. I
While the sorghum cooks, preheat your oven to 400f. Halve the zucchini lengthwise, then halve each half again. Chop the zucchini into ¾ inch chunks. You should have about 1½ -2 cups. Cut the radishes into quarters. Toss the zucchini, radishes, and corn with a tablespoon of olive oil and transfer the vegetables to parchment or foil lined baking sheet. Sprinkle lightly with salt and pepper. Roast the vegetables for 25-30 minutes, stirring them once through, or until the radishes and zucchini are tender and browning slightly. Allow the vegetables to cool for 10 minutes. To prepare the grain salad, mix the sorghum and roasted vegetables together. Whisk together the remaining tablespoon olive oil, mustard, lemon, shallot, salt, and pepper. Pour these ingredients onto the grain and vegetable mixture, then add the chopped basil and tarragon. Toss everything together. Check the salad for seasoning and add extra salt or lemon or pepper as needed. Serve. Leftovers will keep in an airtight container in the fridge for up to three days.
Nutrition information
Serving size: 1¼ cups

Lentils with roasted beets and carrots

Ingredients
2 1/2 cups french lentils (also called puy lentils)
About 1 dozen (1 large bunch) medium-small carrots, with their
tops on
About 1 dozen (2 large bunches) medium-small beets
2 tbsp. olive oil
1/2 cup chopped fresh herbs (whatever you have on hand: basil,
chives, or parsley)
1/2 cup chopped carrot tops
Grated zest of one organic lemon
1/2 cup feta cheese
For eggless aioli:
1/2 cup olive oil
2 cloves garlic
Fresh-squeezed juice of one large lemon (about 1/4 cup)
1/2 tsp. Salt

Directions
Remove the leafy tops from the carrots and beets. Reserve the
carrot tops. (beet greens can also be kept as they are extremely
nutritious and delicious). Wash and scrub the carrots and beets,
removing any soil, leaving their skins on. Place the whole carrots
and beets in a large french oven or enamelled iron pot and mix in
the 2 tbsp. olive oil, fully coating the vegetables in oil.
In a 375 f oven, roast the vegetables for about 30 to 45 minutes,
until tender when pierced with a fork. If you wish, once the beet
are cool enough to handle, you can remove the skins from the
beets by gently rubbing them off with your fingers.
Meanwhile, rinse the lentils and check them for small pebbles,
then place them in a medium saucepan. Cover them with water
and bring to a boil.
Simmer on medium heat, uncovered, for about 30 to 40 minutes,

until tender but not falling apart or turning mushy. (add water if necessary through the cooking). Drain the lentils and place them in a large shallow serving bowl.

In a blender or food processor, puree the garlic, lemon juice, and salt to make the aioli. Add the olive oil and puree until thick and opaque and no chunks of garlic remain. Pour this mixture over the lentils. Add the chopped carrot tops, chopped herbs, and grated lemon zest and toss it all together. Season with a bit of salt and pepper if you wish.

Place the roasted carrots and beets on top, then crumble the feta all around. Serve warm or cold.

Yield: 6-8 servings

Roasted red pepper, cauliflower & walnut buckwheat salad

Yield: 2-3 servings

Ingredients
1 small cauliflower, broken into florets
1 red pepper
2 tbsp olive oil (divided)
1/2 c buckwheat
1/4 c roughly chopped walnuts
1/3 c roughly chopped parsley
1/2 shallot or 1/4 red onion, finely chopped
2 tbsp lemon juice
Salt & pepper

Instructions
Preheat oven to 190c/400f. Toss the cauliflower florets with 1 tbsp of the olive oil, salt and pepper and spread on a baking sheet. Add the whole red pepper to the baking sheet. Roast the vegetables for 20-30 minutes until the cauliflower is brown and crisp at the edges and the pepper is charred and soft (you may

need to remove the cauliflower from the baking sheet and cook the pepper an extra 5 or so minutes).
Chop the red pepper into pieces, removing most of the papery skin. It should come off easily.
Meanwhile, cook the buckwheat. Rinse well then place in a saucepan with 1c water. Bring to the boil, then turn down the heat and leave to simmer, covered for approx 15 minutes. Once all the water is absorbed, turn off the heat and leave to sit, covered, while you prepare the rest of the salad.
Toast the walnuts in a small pan over medium-high heat or on a small baking tray in the oven for approx 5 minutes.
Stir together all the ingredients, including the remaining tbsp of olive oil and season generously with salt and pepper.

Thai peanut curry lentils
serves 5-6

Ingredients
2 cups dry brown lentils
chicken or vegetable broth
1 large onion, sliced thin
1 tbs vegetable oil
1 tsp salt
1 tsp pepper
2 tsp turmeric
1 tsp sugar
1 tsp ground ginger
1/2 tsp garlic powder
2 tsp paprika
1 tsp yellow curry powder
2 tbs yellow curry paste, leveled.
1 can coconut milk
1 tbs peanut butter (preferably all natural)
3 handfuls of fresh spinach

crushed peanuts for garnish (optional)

Directions:

1.Wash The lentils in cold water until the water runs clear (this is very important or the lentils will get "scummy"), put the lentils in a pot with enough broth to cover and simmer covered until lentils tender, about 15 min. (you could just use water but i think broth adds more flavor).

2.While The lentils are cooking: in a large skillet or saucepan, caramelize the onions in the vegetable oil.

3.While The onions are cooking, combine the spices in a separate bowl and mix well. When the onions are cooked, add the spice mixture to the onions and cook over a high heat stirring constantly for 1 to 2 minutes. This "toasts" the spices and brings out the flavors.

4.Stir In the coconut milk and allow the curry base to simmer until the lentils are ready. Add peanut butter and mix to combine. This is your chance to taste your sauce and see if it's to your liking, you may need to add more curry or salt depending on your preferences, remember, the lentils are going to soak up a lot of flavor when you add them in.

5.When The lentils are tender drain them briefly (they should have absorbed most of the water but you don't want the curry to be too watery). Mix the lentil into the curry base then add the spinach and cover over medium heat, the spinach should wilt within a matter of minuets. Serve immediately.

6.I Garnished mine with some chopped peanuts and sriracha for a kick!

*you could uses red or green lentils in place of brown but they might not hold up as well, they tend to have a softer texture than the brown lentils

Buckwheat risotto with mushrooms & hazelnut cream

Yield: 3-4 servings

Ingredients
Hazelnut cream:
1/2 c hazelnuts, soaked overnight
1 c water
1/2 tsp salt
1 tsp lemon juice

Risotto
1 tbsp oil, divided
1 onion, finely chopped
1 clove of garlic, minced
1 tsp chopped fresh thyme or 1/2 tsp dried thyme
1 c buckwheat groats, soaked overnight
1 c vegetable broth
250g/8-9oz chopped mixed mushrooms (i used portobello, chestnut & oyster but use what's available to you)
Salt & pepper
Chopped fresh parsley (optional)

Instructions
For the hazelnut cream
Drain and rinse the hazelnuts then blend in a high-powered blender with 1 c fresh water. Strain through a nut milk bag to get a smooth, white cream. Pour into a small pan, along with the salt and warm gently. Add the dash of lemon juice.

For the risotto:
Heat 1/2 tbsp oil in a pan over medium heat. Add the onion and cook for 5-8 minutes, until translucent. Add the garlic and thyme and cook for a further minute. Drain and rinse the buckwheat well then add to the pan, along with the vegetable broth. Cover, bring

to a boil, then reduce heat and simmer for 10 minutes until all of the liquid has been absorbed.

While the risotto is cooking, heat the remaining 1/2 tbsp of oil in a large frying pan, add the chopped mushrooms, sprinkle with a pinch of salt and cook, stirring occasionally, for 5-10 minutes, until soft.

Add half the mushrooms to the risotto pan, along with the hazelnut cream (reserving a little for drizzling over each plate). Stir and heat for a couple of minutes to warm through.

Check seasoning and serve. Top individual servings with remaining mushrooms, a generous drizzle of hazelnut cream and chopped parsley (if using).

Healing moroccan lentil soup

Yield: 4 bowls or 6 cups
Total time: 50 minutes

Ingredients
1 cup brown lentils*
1 fennel bulb, diced (approx. 3/4 cup)
1 yellow onion, diced (approx. 1 cup)
2 carrots, peeled and chopped (approx. 3/4 cup)
1 sweet potato, peeled and chopped (approx. 2 cups)
3 cloves garlic, minced
1 tablespoon olive oil
2 teaspoons cumin
1 teaspoon turmeric
1/2 teaspoon coriander
1/4 teaspoon cayenne (optional)
1/4 teaspoon cinnamon
6 cups vegetable broth**
Juice of 1 lemon
Salt to taste (if needed)
Fresh cilantro for topping
Thinly sliced radishes for topping (optional)

Method:

Pre heat the oven at 200c/400f/gas 6. Take cubed butternut squash, oil and salt and pepper in a large bowl and mix well. Spread them in a baking tray lined with an aluminium foil and place it on a middle rack of oven and let it roast for 10 minutes. Take it out from the oven and gently mix again and place it on the top rack and let it roast for another 5-10 minutes till it is cooked through.

To roast the butternut squash seeds, simply spread them in a baking tray and place them on a top rack of your oven and let them roast for 3-5 minutes till they turn golden.

While the butternut squash is roasting, wash and cook the masoor dal with turmeric, few drops of oil and 1½ cups of water. Add little water in between if needed and cook till the lentils starts to fall apart, about 10-15 mins.

Take half the amount of roasted butternut squash and add it to the cooked lentils. With a help of stick blender, grind this mixture to smooth. If using food processor or mixer make sure that the dal and squash have cooled little bit. You can also use potato masher to mash lentil and squash mixture. Keep it aside till needed.

Heat oil in a pan and add cumin seeds to it. When it starts to sizzle and turn golden red, add finely chopped onion, garlic and ginger. Sauté till onion turns translucent, about 1-2 mins.

Now add mashed lentil and butternut squash mixture, 2-3 cups of water or vegetable stock and garam masala. Let it cook uncovered for 5-7 minutes. Add salt and pepper to taste and add more water if needed.

Switch off the gas and mix in other half of roasted butternut squash and lemon juice. Serve them hot garnished with roasted butternut squash seeds and spring of coriander leaves and enjoy with freshly baked bread or even tandoori roties

Buckwheat mushroom risotto

Total time-45 min
Serves: 4

Ingredients
1 tbsp extra virgin coconut oil
1.5 cups roasted buckwheat groats
½ onion
6 cups mushrooms
2 cloves garlic
5 cups vegetable broth
1 tbsp + juice from half of a lime
¼ tsp salt (or to taste)
1 tbsp nutritional yeast
2 sprigs thyme
Truffle oil (optional)
Lime zest, parsley, green onion (garnish)

Instructions
Dice the onions, mushrooms, and garlic and sauté over medium-low heat with 1 tbsp coconut oil.
When the onions become translucent and most of the water released from the mushrooms has been evaporated, add the buckwheat groats and toast until a fragrant, nutty aroma is released.
Add 1 cup broth, 1 tbsp of lime juice, salt, and thyme and simmer on low heat, stirring constantly, until most of the liquid has been absorbed. Add another cup of broth, stirring constantly, and wait for the liquid to be absorbed before adding more broth. Repeat process until all 5 cups of broth have been absorbed into the risotto.
Remove from heat and stir in the nutritional yeast and lime zest. Garnish the buckwheat risotto with more lime zest, parsley and diced green onion. Drizzle with leftover lime juice and truffle oil for an added flavor boost.

Cauliflower salad with chickpeas, baby kale, cumin, lemon & toasted buckwheat

Ingredients
2 tsp cumin seeds
1 heaped tsp coriander seeds
1/4 tsp fennel seeds
2 tbsp olive oil
1 onion, finely sliced
2 garlic cloves, minced
1 small cauliflower
Zest and juice of 1 lemon (2 lemons if your lemon is not
particularly juicy)
1 cup cooked chickpeas
2 cups baby kale
1/4 cup buckwheat groats
Salt and pepper

Instructions
Grind the cumin, coriander and fennel in a mortar and pestle as
finely as you can.
Place a large frying pan over a low heat. Add 2 tsp of olive oil
and add the onion, garlic and spices and cook until the onion is
golden and soft. Remove from the heat and place in a large salad
bowl.
Finely chop the cauliflower. I like to use the stalks too, but is up
to you if you prefer to use the florets only. Increase the heat of the
frying pan to medium high and add 1/3 of the remaining oil. Fry
1/3 of the cauliflower until golden and tender. Remove from the
heat and add to the onions. Cook the remaining cauliflower and
place in the bowl with the onions. Add the lemon zest and juice,
along with the chickpeas and toss to combine and leave to cool
completely.
Wash out the frying pan and dry it completely. Place the pan over

a medium heat and add the buckwheat. Toast for 3 to 4 minutes until golden and fragrant. Leave to cool.
Before serving toss through the baby kale and season with salt and pepper. Sprinkle the toasted buckwheat over the top.

Overnight coconut buckwheat porridge
Serves: 2

Ingredients
1 cup buckwheat groats
¼ cup chia seeds
3 cups unsweetened coconut milk (or any other nut milk like almond, rice, soy, etc.)I Used silk brand - not the canned kind
1 cup water
2 teaspoons vanilla extract
¼ teaspoon cinnamon
Pinch of salt
Toppings:
½ cup walnuts (or any other unsalted nuts of your choice)
1 ½ cup berries, pomegranate seeds, etc. (any fresh fruit you have at home)
½ cup unsweetened shredded coconut

Instructions
Mix buckwheat groats, chia seeds, coconut milk, water, vanilla extract, cinnamon, and salt in a bowl. Cover it with stretch film and let it sit overnight in the fridge.
In the morning, place it in a pot, and cook, stirring occasionally, for 7-8 minutes (or until thick and creamy).
Garnish it with fruit, coconut, and nuts. Serve.

Buckwheat risotto with spinach and mushrooms

Total time-35 mins
Serves: 2 to 3

Ingredients
1 small onion, chopped
3 cloves garlic, minced
½ cup buckwheat groats
1 cup mushrooms, sliced
2 cups spinach, shredded
1 green onion, chopped
½ tsp salt, or more to taste
2 cups vegetable stock

Instructions
In a medium-sized pot, sauté the onions and garlic in a bit of water until soft. Add the buckwheat and stir it around until it gets coated by the onions and garlic.
Add the mushrooms and ½ cup of stock and stir. When all the liquid is absorbed, add another ½ cup of stock. Repeat until the buckwheat is tender, or until the stock has been used (you may not need to use all of it, though).
Mix in the spinach, green onion and salt and stir until the spinach has wilted. Taste and adjust seasonings if necessary.

General tso's chickpeas
Total time: 20 mins
Serves: 2-4 servings

Ingredients
For marinating the chickpeas:
1 tb. soy sauce (or tamari for gf)
1 tb. mirin (or dry sherry)
1 and ½ c. cooked chickpeas (equal to 1 15-oz. can), rinsed and drained

For the sauce:
¼ c. + 2 tb. vegetable broth
1 and ½ tb. tomato paste
½ tb. natural peanut butter
1 tb. soy sauce (or tamari for gf)
1 tb. rice vinegar
1 tb. + 1 tsp. coconut sugar (or other sugar)
2 tsp. sriracha or other chili sauce
1 tsp. toasted sesame oil
1 tsp. prepared mustard
1 tsp. cornstarch
⅛ tsp. freshly ground black pepper or white pepper
For the general tso's chickpeas stir-fry:
~1 tb. neutral oil (i used sunflower seed oil)
¼ of a large onion (or 1 shallot), thinly sliced
1 large broccoli crown, cut into florets
1 red bell pepper, cut into thin strips
1 tsp. minced ginger
2 cloves garlic, minced
General tso's sauce (above)
Marinated chickpeas (above)
(optional) green onions, sesame seeds, and fresh red onion, for
serving
(optional) cooked rice, for serving

Instructions
For marinating the chickpeas:
Stir together the soy sauce and mirin in a bowl and add the
chickpeas. Let sit for 10 minutes (i do this first and let them
marinate while i prepare the sauce and veggies).
For the sauce:
Whisk together all of the sauce ingredients and set aside.
For the stir-fry:
If you plan to garnish your dish with extra diced red onion, put
the amount you want for garnish in a small bowl with cold water
now. This will help to mellow out its flavor.
Heat oil in a large skillet over high heat. When the oil is hot, add

the onion, stirring continuously.

Continuing to stir, add the broccoli, bell pepper strips, ginger, and garlic.

Stir in the general tso's sauce. Drain the chickpeas and stir them in too. Cook for 1-2 more minutes, continuing to stir frequently, or until the mixture is hot throughout and the sauce has coated the chickpeas and vegetables. Add more soy sauce or chili sauce to taste.

Serve over rice if desired; garnish as desired with green onions, sesame seeds, and drained soaked red onion from above

Roasted eggplant coconut curry

Total time-45 mins
Serves: 4

Ingredients
1 eggplant, chopped
1 tbsp grapeseed oil (or cooking oil of choice)
3 garlic cloves, peeled and crushed
Salt to taste
1 tbsp coconut oil (or cooking oil of choice)
1 onion, diced
2 tsp (loose) grated ginger
1-15 oz can chickpeas, drained and rinsed
1 heaping cup tomatoes, chopped (i used mixed grape heirloom tomatoes)
1 cup coconut cream or full fat coconut milk
½ cup filtered water
1 tbsp coriander
1 tbsp turmeric
1 tbsp garam masala
½ tsp cinnamon
¼ tsp cardamom
Cayenne pepper to taste
Black pepper to taste

For serving: cooked brown basmati rice, fresh cilantro/basil/scallions

Instructions
Preheat oven to 400°f.
Toss eggplant with grapeseed oil, crushed garlic, and salt and spread on baking sheet. Bake until browned, 20-25 minutes.
Heat coconut oil in a wok or large skillet over medium heat. Add onion and ginger and cook until tender, 5-6 minutes.
Remove eggplant from oven and add to skillet. Stir in chickpeas, coconut cream, tomato, and spices. Cover and simmer about 10 minutes.
Serve over cooked brown basmati rice topped with fresh herbs as desired.

Vegan butter chicken
Total time-30 mins
Serves: 5 servings

Ingredients
2 small yellow onion (or one large), chopped
2 - 3 cloves garlic, minced
2 tsp garam masala
¾ tsp cumin, cinnamon & ginger
¼ - ¾ tsp cayenne pepper
1¼ cup low sodium vegetable broth
2¾ cups plain tomato sauce
1 tbsp coconut sugar or cane sugar*
⅓ cup raw cashews + 3 tbsp to roast for garnish
3 cups chickpeas

Directions
Soak cashews in hot water while preparing the sauce.
On medium high heat, in a large pan, saute the onions and garlic

with the spices (garam masala, cumin, cinammon, ginger and cayenne pepper) in ¼ cup of the vegetable broth until the onions are soft and the spices are fragrant.

Add the remaining vegetable broth (1 cup), plain tomato sauce and sugar. Simmer for 5-8 minutes or so until fragrant.

Rinse your cashews, in a blender or in a separate deep bowl, blend ⅓ cup of raw cashews with about ⅓ cup of the butter chicken sauce that is simmering on the stove until creamy and smooth . I used a stick immersion blender and blended the soaked cashews with a bit of the sauce in a deep bowl. If you are using a high speed blender you may need to add in about ½ cup of the sauce with the cashews for it to blend well. Transfer the blended sauce back into the pan with the rest of the butter chicken sauce. If using, in a separate pan, over medium high heat, roast 3 tbsps of cashews for 5 minutes in a pan (these are the cashews that you will use to garnish the butter chicken with).

Add the chickpeas to the pan. Simmer for an additional 5 - 10 minutes. Serve butter chicken over yellow rice pilafor basmati rice. Garnish with roasted cashews.

Kung pao chickpeas

Ingredients:
For the chickpea marinade
2 tablespoons reduced-sodium soy sauce
2 tablespoons rice wine vinegar
1 lime, juiced and zested
1 tablespoon agave or honey
1 tablespoon organic coconut oil, melted
1 tablespoon arrowroot powder or cornstarch
For the chickpeas
2 tablespoons organic coconut oil
1 (14.5-ounce) can chickpeas, drained and rinsed
1 cup bottled all-natural kung pao sauce (or homemade)
2 – 3 garlic cloves, minced

1 (1-inch) knob fresh ginger, grated
1/2 teaspoon chili flakes or crushed red pepper
For the garnish
1 small bunch green onions, thinly sliced
1 – 2 spicy red jalapeños or thai chili peppers
Cashews, for garnish (optional)
Steamed white rice, for serving

Directions:
In a bowl, combine all the ingredients for the marinade. Add the chickpeas to the marinade, and stir well to coat.
Cover the chickpeas, and allow them to marinate for at least 30 minutes to 1 hour.
To a large pan over medium heat, add the coconut oil, the marinated chickpeas and the remaining ingredients for the chickpeas.
Sauté for about 6 – 8 minutes, until the chickpeas begin to caramelize and brown slightly.
Remove from the heat, and allow the chickpeas to cool slightly.
Serve the warm chickpeas over steamed white rice, and garnish with sliced peppers, cilantro, cashews and green onions.

Buffalo chickpea mac 'n' cheese
Serves: 4

Ingredients
Roasted chickpeas
1- 15 oz. Can of cooked chickpeas, drained & rinsed
¼ c. Your favorite buffalo sauce + 1-2 t. Extra
Ranch sauce
3 t. Vegan mayo
2 t. Plain vegan yogurt
2 t. Raw cashews, soaked for 30 mins or more
1 t. Non-dairy milk
1 tsp. Lemon juice
½ tsp. Onion powder

½ tsp. Garlic salt
¼ tsp. Dried parsley
Pinch of dried dill
Pinch of black pepper
Pinch of salt (if you'd like)
Pasta
2½ c. Dried pasta + water for boiling
1 tube cheddar teese
¾-1 c. Non-dairy milk
Optional: pinch of salt
Optional: 1 t. Vegan butter
2 c. Romaine lettuce, chopped
Optional: 1-2 stalks of celery, chopped

Instructions
Roasted chickpeas
Preheat your oven to 375°f. Toss the chickpeas in the ¼ c. of
buffalo sauce until they are evenly coated. Spread them out on a
baking sheet that is lined with parchment paper.
Bake for 12 minutes, and carefully roll them around with a spoon
to get the other side crispy. Bake for another 12-15 minutes, then
place them back in the bowl and toss with the extra 1-2 t. of
buffalo sauce. Set aside.
Ranch sauce
Place all ingredients in a blender and puree until completely
smooth. This may take a couple of times of pushing the
ingredients around, or adding another tablespoon of non-dairy
milk.
Pour into a cup or squirt bottle and set aside.
Pasta
Cook your pasta according to the instructions on the package,
then drain and rinse with cool water.
Place the noodles back in the pot and set the heat to low-medium.
Add the cheddar teese, non-dairy milk, salt and margarine to the
pot and stir until melted and evenly coated.
Add more non-dairy milk if you'd like a creamier sauce.
Serving

When you're ready to serve, toss the romaine (and optional celery) in with the mac 'n' cheese then plate immediately. Place roughly a ¼ c. of chickpeas on top, then drizzle with a little extra buffalo sauce and a generous drizzling of the ranch sauce. Enjoy!

Vegan creamy kale soup with spicy roasted chickpeas
Serves: 6

Ingredients
For the spicy roasted chickpeas
1-14 oz. can chickpeas, rinsed and drained
1 tbsp. olive oil
½ tsp. cayenne pepper (optional)
¼ tsp. salt
For the creamy kale soup
2 tbsp. olive oil
1 large onion, chopped
5 garlic cloves, minced
8 cups vegetable broth
1 large bunch (about 1½ lb) curly kale
1 cup raw cashews, soaked in water 4-8 hours, rinsed and drained
2 tbsp. white wine vinegar
¼ tsp. salt
¼ tsp. pepper

Instructions
Make the spicy roasted chickpeas
Preheat oven to 400°. Line a baking sheet with parchment.
Place chickpeas, olive oil, cayenne and salt in small bowl. Stir to completely coat chickpeas.
Arrange chickpeas in an even layer on baking sheet. Bake until crispy, about 50 minutes, flipping 2-3 times during baking.

Make the creamy kale soup

Heat olive oil in large saucepan or dutch oven over medium heat. Add onion and garlic. Sauté until onion is softened, about 5 minutes. Add broth and remove from heat while you prepare kale and cashews.

Remove the stems from the kale leaves. Working batches, place kale leaves in food processor bowl. Pulse until very finely chopped. Transfer to pot with broth. Continue until all kale is chopped and has been added to pot.

Place cashews in food processor. Blend until smooth, stopping to scrape down sides of bowl as needed. You can optionally add a bit of broth from the pot in order to get a smooth consistency. Transfer cashew mixture to pot with kale and broth. Stir well. Place over high heat and bring to a low boil. Lower heat and simmer, uncovered, until kale is tender, about 10 minutes.

Add vinegar, salt and pepper. Stir well. Taste and adjust seasonings as needed.

Ladle into bowls and top with roasted chickpeas.

Chickpea curry pot pies

Serves: 3-4

Ingredients
For the pie dough:
1 cup all-purpose flour
½ cup whole-wheat pastry flour
¼ teaspoon salt
4 tablespoons cold vegan "butter", cut into pieces (you can use regular butter as well)
Cold water
For the filling:
1 cup sweet potato, peeled and cubed (or use frozen cubed butternut squash)
2 tablespoons olive oil
1 clove garlic, minced
¼ cup all-purpose flour
2 cups vegetable broth

1 teaspoon curry powder
Sea salt and pepper to taste
1 cup frozen mixed vegetables
½ cup frozen mini-pearl onions
1 cup chickpeas, cooked (i used canned chickpeas)

Instructions
Preheat oven to 400 degrees. Place ramekins on a large baking pan and set aside.
To make dough: whisk together flours and salt in a large bowl. Cut pieces of "butter" into flour mixture until no large pieces remain. (i used my hands!) Mix in 3 to 4 tbs cold water until smooth dough forms. Wrap in plastic wrap, and chill while making filling.

To make filling:
In a small sauce pan, steam cubed sweet potatoes until tender. Drain and set aside.

Meanwhile, in a large skillet, heat olive oil over medium heat. Add garlic and sauté until fragrant. Lower heat and slowly whisk in flour, then slowly whisk in broth. Add curry powder, sea salt and pepper to taste. Simmer on low until a "gravy" like consistency is formed.

In a large bowl, add cooked sweet potato, frozen vegetables, pearl onions and chickpeas. Mix in curry "gravy." Pour mixture evenly into ramekins.

On a floured surface, roll out dough until ⅛ inch thick. Cut out circles to fit over the top of the ramekins. (i used a knife and traced around a small side dish to create a perfect circle)
Cover ramekins with pie crust rounds and pinch sides down using the back of a fork. Pierce top with a knife. Bake for 30-40 minutes or until bubbly and tops are golden brown. Enjoy!

Creamy curried kale and chickpeas

Total time-35 mins
Serves: 6

Ingredients
1 large onion, chopped
4 cloves garlic, chopped
1 tablespoon ginger root, minced, or 1 tsp. powdered ginger
1 teaspoon cumin seeds
2 teaspoons garam masala (see below)
1 teaspoon coriander
1 teaspoon turmeric
1/4 teaspoon red pepper flakes
8 cups chopped kale, packed (1 10-ounce bunch, about 6 ounces
after stems removed)
1/2 cup low-sodium vegetable broth
1 cup unsweetened soymilk or other non-dairy milk
1/4 cup raw cashews
2 tablespoons nutritional yeast, optional
2 tablespoons tomato paste
2 15-ounce cans chickpeas, drained and rinsed well
Salt to taste

Instructions
Heat a large, non-stick skillet over medium-high heat. Add onion
and cook until softened and beginning to brown, 4-5 minutes,
adding water by the tablespoon if needed to prevent sticking. Add
the garlic, ginger, and cumin seeds and cook for 1 minute. Add
the remaining spices and cook for another minute, stirring
constantly to prevent burning.
Reduce heat to medium. Stir in the kale and vegetable broth.
Cover and cook until the kale is bright green and tender, about 5
minutes, stirring occasionally.
While the kale is cooking, put the milk, cashews, nutritional

yeast, and tomato paste in the blender and puree until smooth. When the kale is done, add it to the blender and blend until smooth.

Transfer blended mixture back to the skillet and bring to a simmer. Check seasonings and add more to taste. Stir in chickpeas and continue simmering about 10 minutes. Add salt to taste and serve over basmati rice.

Grains I can have:

+ Amaranth - seed; rich source calcium, iron, & magnesium, potassium & calcium, vitamin C chokes?

+ Buckwheat - seed; not related to wheat; not roasted, nutty related a seed of a grain but of fruit like (& earthy) rhubarb or sorrel. Good source fibers, un roasted magnesium, manganese & phosphorous mild, subtle

+ Corn must be 'whole grain corn'. Corn germ is the nutritious bit

+ Millet - seed; valuable source of fiber & protein, as well as minerals as magnesium, potassium, phosphorous & zinc. White, yellow, gray, red. Light nutty flavour

+ Oats - must be hulled & then steamed in kiln before processed into rolled oats, steel cut oats, oatmeal, or oat flour. Carbohydrates & fiber; manganese, phosphorous, magnesium, iron, & zinc. More protein & healthy fats than other grains. Pkgs must say gluten-free

+ quinoa - same family as sugar beets & spinach. Complete protein, nearly twice as much fiber as other grains & excellent source of iron, magnesium, vitamin B2 & manganese

+ Rice - more than 100 varieties grown. Brown has more vitamins & minerals — like manganese, magnesium & copper — than white. Rich in fiber & help lower cholesterol

+ Sorghum — good source carbohydrates, fiber, healthy fat & protein, sorghum also contains vitamins & minerals like magnesium, copper & iron.

In flour form, likened to that of wheat, a good alternative for baking. When cooked in grain fo nutty flavour & chewy texture. Also can be popp as kernels of corn

+ Teff — might be tiniest whole grain on earth, but eac seed packed full of nutrients — including protein, fiber, iron & calcium

Most commonly found in its brown variety, can be prepared in much same way as quinoa & rice, or made into porridge, but due to its size cooks much faster. Also avail as flour, lending mild flavor well to certain breads & foods that contain rich spices